GCSE PHYSICS

EXAM REVISION NOTES

This notebook will help you structure your revision as you prepare for any assessments you have while studying GCSE or IGCSE Physics.

Watching videos is great (and I have hundreds available on my website and YouTube channel) but to understand the content **YOU** need to take an active part in **YOUR** revision.

This book has pages that allow you to structure your revision, with space for you to write in definitions, equations, short topic summaries and the key practical experiments.

It is suitable for all exam boards and, by scanning the QR codes with your phone, you can access additional videos where I show you how to use this notebook.

Don't forget that you can easily find plenty of resources on my GCSE Physics website - including hundreds of additional videos covering the whole course. You can sign up for an individual Premium Plan or ask your teacher about a School Subscription to access this extra material.

Good luck in your exams this year!

Lewis Matheson

Physics Online

GCSE/IGCSE PHYSICS

scan this to find out more —

Your Name

Exam Board

Course Code

Exam Dates

Other Key Dates

Useful Resources   www. gcse physics online. com

EXAM STRUCTURE

how to fill in this page →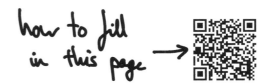

Exam:

Time:

Marks available:

Equipment needed:

Topics covered:

EXAM STRUCTURE

EXAM STRUCTURE

EXAM STRUCTURE

DEFINITIONS

Half-life

The half-life of a radioactive isotope is the time it takes for the number of nuclei of the isotope in a sample to halve.

DEFINITIONS

DEFINITIONS

DEFINITIONS

DEFINITIONS

DEFINITIONS

DEFINITIONS

DEFINITIONS

EQUATIONS

force = mass × acceleration

(Newton's 2nd Law)

$$F = m\,a$$

N   kg   m/s^2

EQUATIONS

EQUATIONS

EQUATIONS

EQUATIONS

EQUATIONS

EQUATIONS

EQUATIONS

EQUATIONS

EQUATIONS

EQUATIONS

EQUATIONS

MATHS FOR PHYSICS

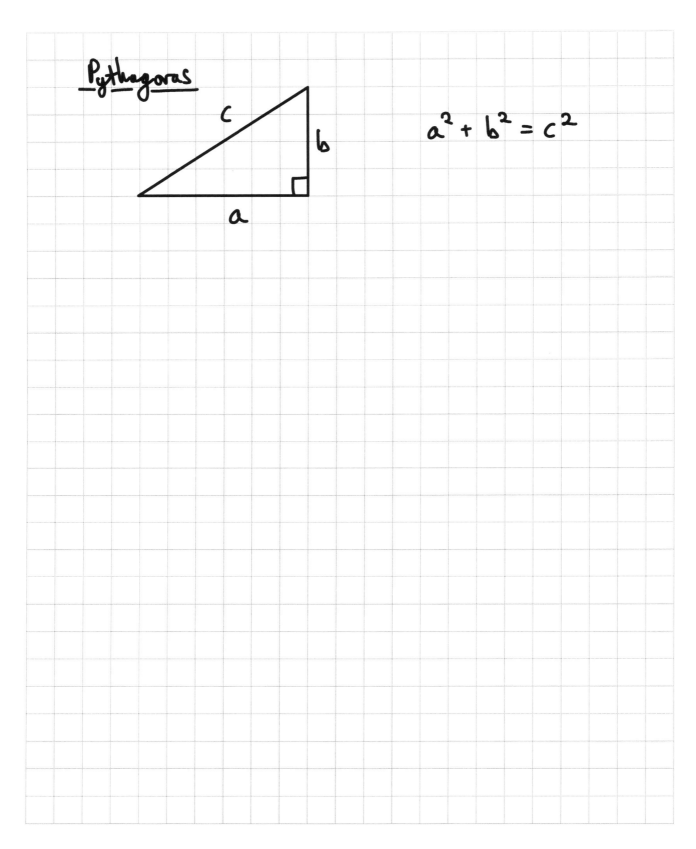

Pythagoras

$$a^2 + b^2 = c^2$$

MATHS FOR PHYSICS

MATHS FOR PHYSICS

MATHS FOR PHYSICS

MATHS FOR PHYSICS

MATHS FOR PHYSICS

GRAPHS

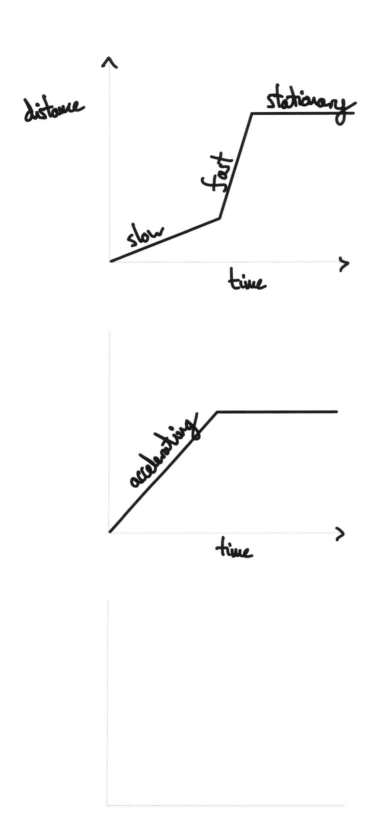

GRAPHS

GRAPHS

GRAPHS

GRAPHS

GRAPHS

GRAPHS

GRAPHS

GRAPHS

GRAPHS

GRAPHS

GRAPHS

GRAPHS

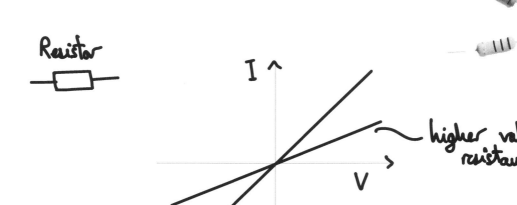

Resistor

higher value of resistance

NOTE The gradient is not equal to $\frac{1}{R}$

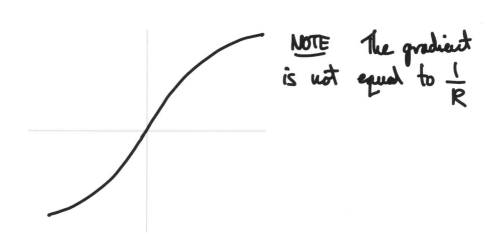

GRAPHS

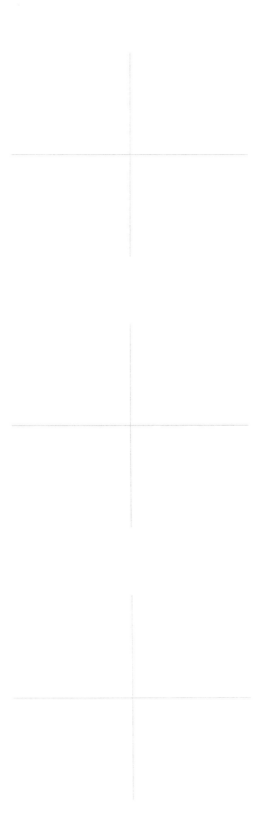

PRACTICAL EXPERIMENTS

Title Hooke's Law (stretching a spring)

Equipment and Diagram

retort stand — spring — slotted masses

Measurements

Mass (mass balance)

Initial length and total length (ruler)

Graphs and Key Equations

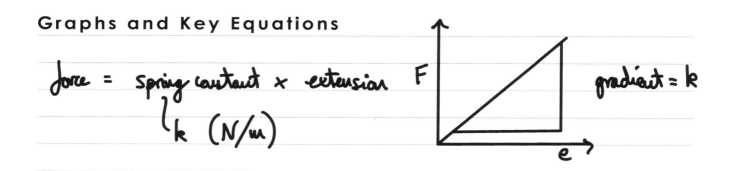

force = spring constant × extension

$\downarrow$ k (N/m)

gradient = k

Typical Results

Depending on the spring used, $k \approx 25 \, N/m$

Hazards and Safety Measures

Spring could flick into your eye

Wear safety glasses to protect your eyes

PRACTICAL EXPERIMENTS

spring from the last practical!

↓

Title

_____

_____

Equipment and Diagram

Measurements

_____

_____

_____

Graphs and Key Equations

_____

_____

_____

_____

_____

Typical Results

_____

_____

Hazards and Safety Measures

_____

_____

PRACTICAL EXPERIMENTS

Title

Equipment and Diagram

Measurements

Graphs and Key Equations

Typical Results

Hazards and Safety Measures

PRACTICAL EXPERIMENTS

Title

Equipment and Diagram

Measurements

Graphs and Key Equations

Typical Results

Hazards and Safety Measures

PRACTICAL EXPERIMENTS

Title

Equipment and Diagram

Measurements

Graphs and Key Equations

Typical Results

Hazards and Safety Measures

PRACTICAL EXPERIMENTS

Title

Equipment and Diagram

Measurements

Graphs and Key Equations

Typical Results

Hazards and Safety Measures

PRACTICAL EXPERIMENTS

Title

Equipment and Diagram

Measurements

Graphs and Key Equations

Typical Results

Hazards and Safety Measures

PRACTICAL EXPERIMENTS

Title

Equipment and Diagram

Measurements

Graphs and Key Equations

Typical Results

Hazards and Safety Measures

PRACTICAL EXPERIMENTS

Title

Equipment and Diagram

Measurements

Graphs and Key Equations

Typical Results

Hazards and Safety Measures

PRACTICAL EXPERIMENTS

Title

Equipment and Diagram

Measurements

Graphs and Key Equations

Typical Results

Hazards and Safety Measures

PRACTICAL EXPERIMENTS

Title

Equipment and Diagram

Measurements

Graphs and Key Equations

Typical Results

Hazards and Safety Measures

PRACTICAL EXPERIMENTS

Title

Equipment and Diagram

Measurements

Graphs and Key Equations

Typical Results

Hazards and Safety Measures

PRACTICAL EXPERIMENTS

Title

Equipment and Diagram

Measurements

Graphs and Key Equations

Typical Results

Hazards and Safety Measures

PRACTICAL EXPERIMENTS

Title

Equipment and Diagram

Measurements

Graphs and Key Equations

Typical Results

Hazards and Safety Measures

PRACTICAL EXPERIMENTS

Title

Equipment and Diagram

Measurements

Graphs and Key Equations

Typical Results

Hazards and Safety Measures

PRACTICAL EXPERIMENTS

Title

Equipment and Diagram

Measurements

Graphs and Key Equations

Typical Results

Hazards and Safety Measures

PRACTICAL EXPERIMENTS

Title

Equipment and Diagram

Measurements

Graphs and Key Equations

Typical Results

Hazards and Safety Measures

PRACTICAL EXPERIMENTS

Title

Equipment and Diagram

Measurements

Graphs and Key Equations

Typical Results

Hazards and Safety Measures

PRACTICAL EXPERIMENTS

Title

Equipment and Diagram

Measurements

Graphs and Key Equations

Typical Results

Hazards and Safety Measures

PRACTICAL EXPERIMENTS

Title

Equipment and Diagram

Measurements

Graphs and Key Equations

Typical Results

Hazards and Safety Measures

DIAGRAMS

Refraction

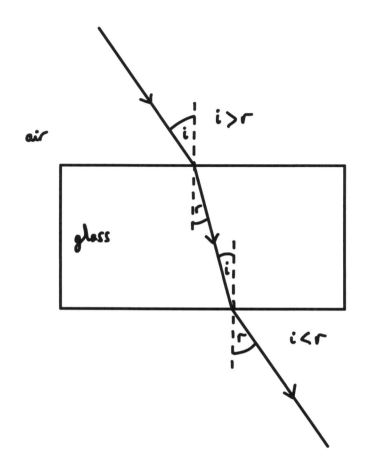

air

glass

i > r

i < r

DIAGRAMS

DIAGRAMS

DIAGRAMS

DIAGRAMS

DIAGRAMS

DIAGRAMS

DIAGRAMS

DIAGRAMS

DIAGRAMS

TOPIC SUMMARY

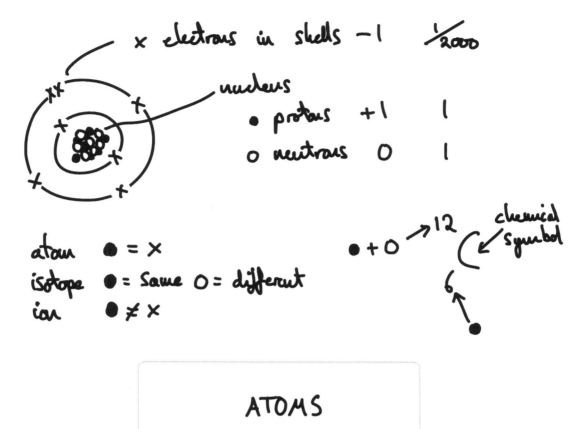

x electrons in shells −1   1/2000

nucleus
- • protons   +1   1
- o neutrons   0   1

• + o → 12   chemical symbol

atom   • = x
isotope   • = same   o = different
ion   • ≠ x

ATOMS

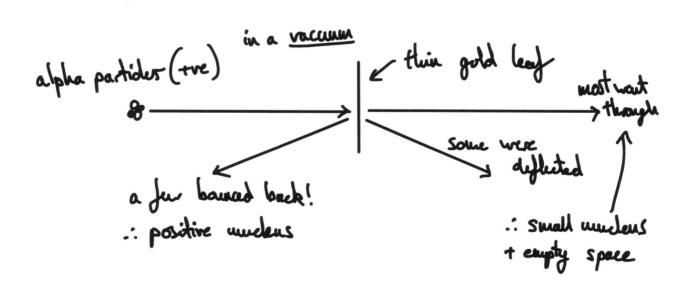

in a <u>vacuum</u>

alpha particles (+ve)   ← thin gold leaf

most want through

a few bounced back!
∴ positive nucleus

some were deflected

∴ small nucleus + empty space

TOPIC SUMMARY

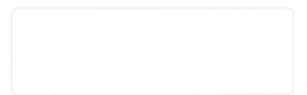

TOPIC SUMMARY

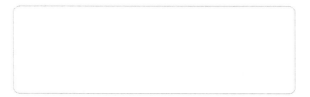

TOPIC SUMMARY

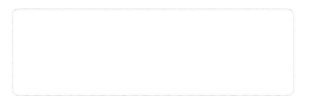

TOPIC SUMMARY

TOPIC SUMMARY

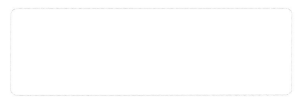

TOPIC SUMMARY

TOPIC SUMMARY

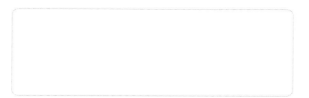

TOPIC SUMMARY

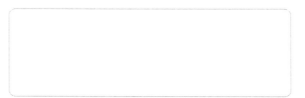

TOPIC SUMMARY

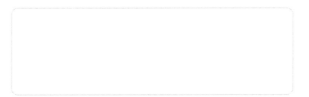

TOPIC SUMMARY

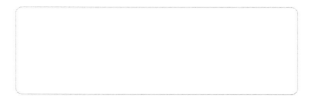

TOPIC SUMMARY

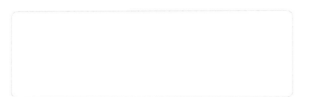

TOPIC SUMMARY

TOPIC SUMMARY

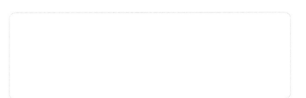

TOPIC SUMMARY

TOPIC SUMMARY

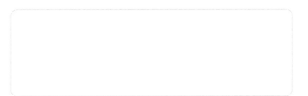

TOPIC SUMMARY

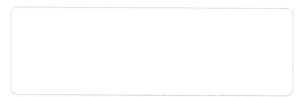

TOPIC SUMMARY

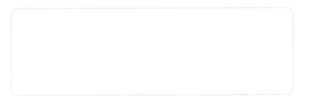

TOPIC SUMMARY

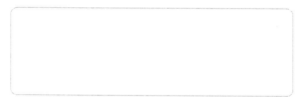

TOPIC SUMMARY

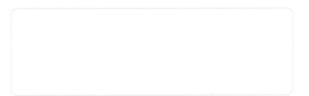

TOPIC SUMMARY

TOPIC SUMMARY

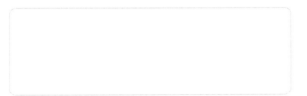

TOPIC SUMMARY

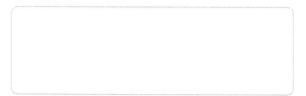

TOPIC SUMMARY

TOPIC SUMMARY

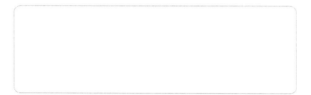

TOPIC SUMMARY

TOPIC SUMMARY

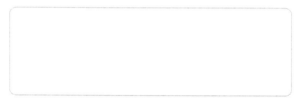

TOPIC SUMMARY

TOPIC SUMMARY

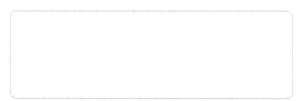

TOPIC SUMMARY

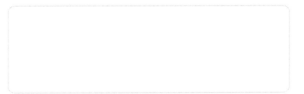

OTHER NOTES

OTHER NOTES

OTHER NOTES

OTHER NOTES

OTHER NOTES

OTHER NOTES

OTHER NOTES

OTHER NOTES

OTHER NOTES

OTHER NOTES

OTHER NOTES

OTHER NOTES

OTHER NOTES